Lord, Did You Really Send Me To That Church?!

B. L. Davis

Copyright © 2012 Beverly L. Davis

All Scriptures used are taken from the King James Version of the Bible.

All rights reserved. No part of this book may be reproduced in any form or by any means without the written permission of the author.

ISBN: 1478297468
ISBN-13:978-1478297468

DEDICATION

To my daughters
Clare, Daphne, Adrien, and Angela
~~~
My Grandkids
Rachel and Dylan
~~~
My Church Family
~~~
My Siblings
~~~
My deceased Godly parents
Deacon Moutry Sr. and Rev. Missionary Bessie Montgomery

This a personal experience of soul searching to help all Christians in these troubled times when Pastors are falling and they don't know in whom to trust.

God has the answers.

God's plans are sometimes

Hard to bear

But as we learn Him__ One thing

Becomes crystal clear;

His love outweighs all we say and do

And unlike us

He is always TRUE. Always! Always!

I believe that at one time or another, most Christians have looked up to heaven and said, "Lord, did you really give me these pastors?" or "did you really send me to this church?" or "was it me you meant or was it someone else with the same name?"

Be honest. You know you did this and probably more. I have found myself close to the brink of really questioning the mind of God, inadvertently, by wallowing in my feelings about what I felt was---unreasonable handling of my Pastors.

Let's be honest saints. Have you felt that your Pastor or Pastors (God help those of us who have two—smile) have flipped their spiritual ever-loving minds and gone to the dark side sometimes?

It's bad enough dealing with a church full of people who joyfully give their life to the Lord then a few years down the road, they are not only on the dark side, but the force that is with them is almost scared of them, *on dark side*. And besides that, they want your job in the church. And guess what sometimes the Pastors *gives it to them*.

Then sometimes during your Christian walk, it seems like your Pastor has lost all reasoning. It has happened people! What is going on you say? What is happening? I want to share some of what I've learn and what I've been taught by Holy Spirit over the years.

Life is never what you plan it to be, even in Christ. You will learn this as you yield your old nature and grow in the Lord.

When you want to be mad, you can't be. When you plan to walk out and quit-- Holy Spirit won't let you. And if you do walk- things are never the same. If you are one of those who have walked away from a previous ministry without God's approval, you know--- things are never the same. You lose your *Peace* and *Joy*.

All that hard fought territory you gained from the devil—poof—it's all gone. You are almost back to ground ZERO.

You can front all you want to, but you are just living a lie in denial.

God has a purpose and plan for each of us. That includes a coming together in a house of worship: with a particular Sheppard or Sheppard's, if he gives you a husband and wife team- to feed you while you live your life here on earth.

God knows what he is doing. You can't repent on your own or grow yourself spiritually. You can't even mature on your own. And you definitely can't fight the devil on your own.

He'll tear you apart and everyone near and kin to you. God equips Pastors to raise and protect their sheep. They have been specially anointed from God for this task.

"And I will give you Pastors according to my own heart, which shall feed you with knowledge and understanding." Jer. 3:15

Who can know the mind of God but those He chose to give it to. And with that kind of knowledge, YOU CAN NOT MATURE YOURSELF. Go to church. Ask God for that right church and he will give it to you.

Not forsaking the assembling of ourselves together, as the manner of some is; but exhorting one another… (Heb 10:25). There is a place of worship for everyone, according to their temperament. God knows each of us.

God wants you in the right church…but don't be deceived by deceiving yourself. Churches can't save you only Jesus can save. Only the Word of God can save you. A Pastor who is God's Sheppard to us here on earth, help us to grow in the Grace and Mercy of His Word.

A place to assemble is where we give God the praise and come together for strength and growth. We must have this.

Jesus taught from a focal point to a crowd...not to one or two at a time. He came to minister to the people. He had the temple also. They just would not accept His teaching in the Temple.

God has a reason for everything He does.

Everything He gives us...including a Pastor... and a Church.

We need spiritual help beyond ourselves and a sanctuary from the world...a place apart from unbelievers where we can come and be refreshed and renewed. To fellowship.

As one...connected together we find strength when we feel sick and tire of always going through and seeing others less faithful to God getting by.

You need a Pastor that you can connect with. Relate to. If you are a bubbly person, then a quiet sedate Pastor might make you feel that you are too loose and you might be uncomfortable going to them. You might think, that they think, you are a dizzy head. But that is just your personality. Some Pastors are very up-beat in their personality. So quiet people might feel a little turn off and over-whelmed.

This is true. Real world truth.

But because God cares about each and every one of us, he will fulfill (some) of our needs. Some natural and All spiritual.

He wants us to be happy in Him so why would he not for-fill our spiritual needs. We can't survive have equip.

Jesus wants us to have Joy in Him some where we worship is important to Him.

He made each of us different. Our personalities, wants and desires are all different. So why would we underestimate what God would or would not do for us.

It is vital to be in the right church with the right Pastor. If He led you to that church it is for your good. If you have been bucking against Holy Spirit speaking to you about where you are; just man up or woman up; confess and ask Holy spirit to help you.

We don't all act the same, but a lot of people act similar. So Holy Spirit would not send you to a place of quiet worship if you are a bubbly, lively person. He will consider YOU and what YOU need.

So that means God will give you the type of Pastor that you need for your personality and the type of church you attend will be ideal.

I will also say something that may sound controversial, but from my observations in my nearly sixty years of age, and in over twenty years as a Christian teacher, and thirteen years as a minister, I will make this statement:

I've visited Caucasian churches and from my observing of these church services, and on TV, and from comments of white co-workers over the years, God give different pastors for different churches, and Caucasian Pastors totally fit the more quieter services that African-American church don't usually have.

Now there is always the exception to the rules. So we do see Caucasian churches, especially those with mixed congregations, much more vocal, and fiery then in those that are pre-80's on.

If African-American Christians are honest, before cable TV churches and God doing a new thing in these end-times, we considered Caucasian Christian services to be as close to too quiet as it could come; and not lively enough for a brother or sister. Who can say—boring! But no—more—NO MORE!

We are living in exciting times. Caucasian churches have put an end to that lie about dry. Yes they have. The spirit fill churches today have no ethnic labels. It's all about the Spirit. It is not about the dignified Methodist or the traditional Baptist. Or the Holy Rollers who think they have the only game in town. It is about being filled with the life of JESUS. That Pentecostal experience that Luke wrote about in the book of Acts 2:1-4. It's about that FIRE in the BELLY.

We didn't fight to integrate the churches. Way back then, we liked our Sunday mornings services where we could jump, stomp, sing to the top of our lungs, and sweat the house down. Then go in the back and get a plate of food to take home. That was CHURCH folks!

Good heavens, what black pastor was about to limit his sermon to just thirty minutes. It took thirty minutes for just one "Yeahhhhhhhhhhhhhhhhh" to be said.

Back to the topic. Smile. LoL

So, back to what I was saying about a pastor for a church. When you run across a white pastor that can, 'lay it down', then we say, *"can't he can preach*...On TV when you see a white preacher throwing down, then you can bet that there will be black folks sitting in the pews in that church. They are attracted to what they are *use* to. He sounds like a black man." What is this saying, that the majority of black people like lively, upbeat music? Or are they conditioned to tradition. It seemed like- in the past- about all the white churches I visited or saw on TV- they liked quieter music—hymns etc… and the pastor's sermons were not two or three hours long. You know-short and sweet; 30 minutes or less. But as my eyes became more open spiritually, I saw more, naturally. Sometimes a 30 minute punch-knockout-was all it took. Long is not always better. Loud is not always what's needed.

God's people need to be taught. In a quiet atmosphere-you can hear so much being said. You can ingest the Word that can sustain you when the hollering is all over and done with.

Now there are always exceptions to every rule. So make sure that the Pastor God sent you to, is the one He sent you to, and not the one you followed because dad, mom, girlfriend, boyfriend, or unhappiness led you there.

It's amazing some reasons why people join churches. For example:

1. Food. They have a kitchen and prepare food every Sunday.

2. Money. They have a charity that helps with utilities or burnouts, or the homeless or the lazy.
3. Child Care. A free place to dump the kiddies. Free child care while mummy and daddy lay up on Sunday morning.
4. Singles. A place to find a date in the singles ministries. A good fresh church girl with no disease. Not played over too much. And hopefully no babies he got to feed.
5. Control. A place to come and bully and control a captive crowd.
6. Thieves. A place to come get a position in finances and steal the God-fearing honest tithe payers' money. A wolf in sheep clothing.
7. Sexual predators. Looking for victims. Older lonely women. Young women looking for their Boaz. Young girls and boys they can molest in the back rooms in Jesus name. Destroying their lives

Yes these seven things are real. Read the newspapers. Check out the arrest sections on your computer. Ask older people who have been alive for a while.

The church attracts all types. Make sure you have the pastor that you can relate to. That you can open up to. If you don't like your pastor, how in glory name will you ever be able to go to him or her, with a problem? Get real folks!

People, you better ask God for a Sheppard who can:

- Watch out for your soul.

- Pray for your soul.
- Who can lay hands on you in agreement and hear from Heaven.
- See the wolf coming in the midnight hour to steal, kill, and destroy.
- Not in it for your money
- Looking for fame

If you are afraid of your pastor, how can he or she ever be a positive influence in your life? You can't trust what you fear.

If you want to be at a church for status sake- say for instance- because you are black, and the white church is influential. But you grew up in a Baptist church where some fire was falling and the choir sung <u>Hot, Hot</u> songs. You might start to feel conflicted because on Sunday morning a hymn is not enough. If that thirty minute sermon didn't do what pastor Rob's hour long Baptist sermon did, guess what, you are a hypocrite in the spirit. But you are willing to be a hypocrite for status sake.

So you go home lacking what you need to sustain your spirit man during that coming week. God forbid you have a weak moment—you don't have any strength to fight. Then you are ashamed to go to your Pastor or Pastors to ask for help or confess. Because you show that you are out of place in the spirit and out of place with God. That you know you are in the wrong church or that that Pastor is not for filling a Sheppard's need in your life.

So you sit, weak, back-slidden. Unhappy. No good to

God or man. But don't want to make that change.

Listen up people. Your soul is at stake!!!

If you do not leave feeling what Holy Spirit meant for you to feel. What Jesus gave his life for you to feel is:

- Peace
- Love
- Victory
- Strength
- Determination to fight the good fight

Then you didn't get what God meant for you to receive from him through your Pastor/ Pastors.

We are cheating ourselves but especially Jesus who died for us.

There is quiet worship for some; lively worship for others; and a combination of the two some worshippers.

Some people like a preacher that teaches in a meditative teach style. They don't want their Pastor busting a sweat.

They like dignify worship. Calm exegesis of the Word. That is the kind of Pastor traditionally white Pastors are known to be. Some are changing this as we see on cable TV. They are about the Word and they bring and it seems like they intend to bring the roof down with them. Smile yea!!!

There is nothing wrong with this type of worship. Jesus taught the Word. But the Word must be taught with life: *With the Anointing of the Holy Spirit.* Not dry and dead.

Jesus said, *"I am come that they might have Life, and that they might have it more abundantly" John 10:10.*

When someone dies--- Their body is lifeless. But a body that is alive shows signs of life-activity-energy-purpose. Dead is dead and LIFE IS LIFE PEOPLE! If you are born again you have been given new life. You have the activity of your SPIRITUAL LIMBS, so use them. Even in quiet worship there is life.

1 Thessalonians 4:17 says that *"we will be caught up to meet the Lord in the air."* that sounds like activity to me. That sounds like a surge of power and energy taking place. A dead body can't respond to that call; unless it's the dead in Christ, and then Holy Spirit will reanimate the dead to life again.

I use to prefer quiet sermons to what I grew up with in the Pentecostal Movement. But now I see I can have it both ways because God gave me exactly what I needed---a combination of the two. With Pastors who deliver TEACHING and PREACHING as Holy Spirit leads and guides them. God gave the 5 fold Ministry because we need all 5.

Some people try to escape by hiding in dead churches where nothing is required of them. Not allegiance to God, or Pastor, the congregations, or the church.

They don't have to change their life living or make any commitments to being a witness for Jesus. They don't have to say "praise-em- or wave their hands"

There are no altar calls or call for anything but tithes and committee selections.

Make sure that you go where God send you. Whether you are white are black, brown or green.

Sometimes our white brothers and sisters in Christ come to us because they want to cross over and show that they can adapt, but they look out of place and it shows in their demeanor. They love the Lord and they love their black brothers and sisters, but the type of service and preaching just does not resonate with them.

Be who you are. Go where Holy Spirit send you. There is a church for everyone: whether you are Black, White, Hispanic, Asian or White.

But wherever you are, you have an obligation to give God your best. Serve Him with all your heart. Make sure that the Pastor is a Pastor after God's own heart.

All you have to do is ask Holy Spirit to lead and guide you to where you need to go. Then be prepared to be a sheep after you get there.

I'll say that again. Be prepared to be a *SHEEP AFTER YOU GET THERE*.

Sheep don't lead a Shepherd. Nowhere in the Bible- or do you see on a movie—or TV, where the Shepherd is behind- and the sheep is ahead with the staff in the hooves leading; whacking the Sheppard on his legs to keep him straight or to hurry him on.

Think about that!

But in some churches that's exactly the case. "Mr. Pastor I didn't like that sermon-WHACK!!! You preached too long-WHACK!!!"

"I'm a Deacon and you know I got a woman on the side- why did you preach that sermon-WHACK!!! WHACK!!!

When you arrive to where God is sending you, if you are not going to be the Pastor, you are a sheep with no other rights but sheep rights. Baa! Baa!

I believe that the type of Pastor you have and where you worship is vital to your mental, and your emotional well being.

But when you are sitting in a church and you feel like running up to the pulpit and grabbing the Pastor and doing some un-heavenly damage on him or her, in the midst of their deliverance of the Word of the Lord------WELL

Well something's wrong--- Don't you agree? Many of you reading this know this to be true! We've had ungodly thoughts because we were sitting in the pews mad with the Pastor.

Guess what? You could have been validated in some of your anger. You might have been done wrong; or been misunderstood. All you might have meant was good for the Pastor and good for the church, but it didn't turn out that way.

And all of your explaining didn't help. Guess what? We are human; Bishops and Pastors on down! Nobody is perfect! If you feel that you have been misunderstood, go to

God.

He heals all hurts. He soothes all pains. He dries all tears.

"But thou, O Lord, art a shield for me; my glory, and the lifter up of my head. I cried unto the Lord with my voice, and he heard me out of his holy hill. Selah. I laid me down and slept; I awaked; for the Lord sustained me" Psalm 3:3-5.

But Jesus will not uphold you thinking or feeling evil towards your Pastors. If you are guilty right now-repent for He is ever faithful to forgive us our sins. Make it right with God.

If your Pastors are not right---God will deal with them. You think that the one who holds the Universe in His hands can't correct minor human errors? The devil is a liar and the truth is not in him.

If you are where you are suppose to be and with the Pastor(s) God gave you, there is nothing Holy Spirit will not perfect. You can leave it all up to Him.

But if you are where you are supposed to be, with the right Pastors that God sent you to, then God will speak to those Pastors, if they need to be spoken to.

You as a sheep do not; do not; correct your Pastors. Give them a piece of your mind. Go to their homes for a talk. That's not your place. God calls Pastors and he speaks to them. Not Sheep correcting Pastors!

Ephesians chapter 4 verses 10-12 states: *"He that descended is the same also that ascended up far above all heavens, that he might fill all things and he gave some, Apostles, and some, prophets; and some evangelists; and some pastors and teachers; for the perfecting of the saints, for the working of the ministry, for the edifying of the body of Christ."*

If you think God made a mistake and put you in the wrong place, you go to him. But do it before you act like a fool and get put out of the church or walk out in bad standing.

Then you are living under a curse.

"Touch not mine anointed and do my prophets no harm" Psalm 105:15.

The problem so often is that many Pastors are not God sent Pastors. They were not called by God.

They decided they want to be a Pastor because it looks good; pays good; prestige or just want to help.

Some are told, and I've heard this all my life, your head's shape like a preacher. You look like a preacher. Or, some people just don't want to be told what to do. They will start a church with their wife, children and pets in their yards, before they sit under another man or woman and be lead.

They refuse to be a follower. They are not leaders; whatever they might delude themselves into believing. But they refuse to help build up the body of Christ simply because they don't want to be submissive to another.

On Sunday mornings you can see hundreds of storefronts and small churches with three or four cars.

And that's all you see every Sunday when you pass by. This is a sad state of affairs. But satan is happy. He loves division. A hundred separate fronts are better than one or two united fronts.

Right!

The internet is flowing with ads for ministry licenses for any type of ministry degree you want. If you got the money—you got the degree, and God has nothing to say in any of it. There are more PhD's in the ministry than a person can count.

One minute you are introduced to a minister and the next time you meet him or her it's Dr. So and So.

Jesus wept and He's still weeping over man's stupidness.

When a man or a woman is not happy where he or she is. Or--they are where God did not send them--they can end up filled with bitterness in the church. Then they leave and take these spirits with them and contaminate other weak souls where ever they go if they are not delivered.

Or they stay and we have this:

- Sheep with a congregation within the church that the Pastors have no idea exist.
- *Sheep counseling sheep*. But I can say this about our church. Not in my church and our Pastors get wind of it.

Besides, Holy Spirit keeps them up on the latest. They don't have any snitches. They get on their faces, and Holy

Spirit keeps them informed.

I almost made a foolish mistake and left because I felt my Pastors had made a decision that was unjust. I felt their decision was too hard for me to bear for what I felt was just a misunderstanding; an honest mistake.

I was really upset. I did not disrespect my Pastors though, but I felt hurt and let down after all my work for our ministry over the years.

Sometimes we only see with natural eyes- when we should always-always see with spiritual eyes. But human emotions are human emotions and that is why we need Jesus.

My Pastors came to me and spoke to me in love--even though I wasn't feeling that love at that time. True Pastors love their sheep and will fight for them. They won't just let them walk away and be sifted by life and the devil, nor by their own foolish decisions. That is how you can tell the real deal from the phony.

But Holy Spirit spoke to my heart because I knew to go to Him. I knew to go to my Father in Heaven; to Jesus my Lord and cry my hurt out to them. If you truly have Holy Spirit on board He will never leave you. And when the pity party is over---He'll come in that quiet time and speak to you.

Then we can go to our Pastors. Not to sheep who need a savior themselves. Not to the internet for your "friends" to encourage you. Not even for Bishops or Pastors or Evangelists on the internet to counsel you. But After God— your Pastors are next in your chain of spiritual command.

I cried out to God and I said Lord, I believe I was done wrong. This is what I believe. Lord help me! If I'm wrong help me to see different; because Lord I don't see it.

After my heart had a time to settle Holy Spirit reminded me of this:

"For unto whomsoever much is given, of him much shall be required: and to whom men have committed much, of him they will ask the more" St Luke 12: 48.

As a minister, God has called me to a higher standard. If I want to be punished like laity, not a minister, then I should give up being a minister. I was called to help feed God's sheep. If I want to be a help to the Pastors in the call I was called in---Teacher in the Five-Fold Ministry---then I need to be held to a different-higher standard than laity.

I must take my corrections quicker and even the more humble than the ones sitting in the pews.

I have to be that example that God says he needs. You can't lead if you can't follow. You can't correct if you can't be corrected.

A minister is a minister, but they are still a sheep, subject unto the Pastor. Who are subject unto God!

As I allowed Holy Spirit to show me, me, I saw that I needed to change some things in myself.

I realized that God will allow circumstances to happen to help you see faults in yourself. Faults that causes us to not want to be:

- Shamed
- Rebuked
- Corrected

You will say: "I don't have any serious faults." *Especially if you are clergy.* "Not me!" But that is exactly what it is. We are constantly going on toward perfection. But until we die, we struggle against the flesh that can never be saved. And when Holy Spirit wants you to grow to another level, and you feel like you are just going strong, no problems—God will allow a situation to arise, to happen-- and you will have to face some ugly truths about yourself.

You will see just how spiritual you really are.

That's why God gives you that Pastor. And No-- he did not make a mistake--because you needed to grow. You needed to know what is inside of you so that you can grow spiritually, and be not deceived.

I stayed and I love my Pastors even the more. I don't understand everything they do and say. And I probably won't be happy with every decision they make. But as I teach, it's not about carnal understanding. It's about Holy understanding.

We can't fully understand God's mind. So we can't fully understand how he uses the men and women he places over us neither. But we do know that he makes NO mistakes. Some things are just a matter of acceptance. The same way we accept that the sun is in the sky and the stars will shine at night. We must accept that God has our best interest at heart. Ask Him to give you that Pastor and church that you will need all the days of your life.

It is all a matter of trusting God. Trusting His decisions in who he calls to leadership in His churches. Then going forth and assisting those leaders that He has given us.

Always lean on your Helper, Holy Spirit, if you don't understand something. Be careful of your words. Words can be repented but not erased from memory.

Remember your Pastor is only a man or woman. They are different because God made them different by making them *Shepherds*. Honor what God has done and He will bless you.

I felt lead to write this book because I know someone will be helped by these words.

Pray for all Pastors. Their labor is hard and sometimes unthankful from their members. Pray for all ministers who God call to aid the churches in the Five-Fold Ministries. Pray that God bless this book as it goes into the hands of the ones who need to read it.

I started writing this book in November of 2009; the same year of so many of the mighty tests that I went through. I finished this book in March of 2010. I've wanted it to be published ever since. I thought 2011 would be the year but now is the time.

May God Bless and keep you.

Wisdom

By Elder B. L. Davis

My Lord I will trust in your Wisdom
Your strength is enough for me
I've learned hard lessons from life
But you are the author of my life
I've learned my lessons well.

In You

By Elder B. L. Davis

Eyes see, fingers touch
Spirit blend with spirit
My Lord my God in you I trust
Ease my fears hold my tears
I believe in you I hold you dear

Beyond

By Elder B. L. Davis

Can you still see me Lord
Beyond your many stars
Beyond the myriad clusters
Of galaxies, Jupiter, and Mars?

I seem so small and insignificant
A mote; a speck; a thought
In infinities scale
Do a Great God's thoughts go so far?

I can only hold and trust
And pray and hope in your Word
That when I cry out to you
In your promise I will be heard.

ABOUT THE AUTHOR

Beverly Davis lives in South Carolina with two of her daughters and their pet cat Rufus. She graduated from Francis Marion University with a BA in English and Collaterals in Professional and Creative Writing. She worked for over 15 years in the education system. Beverly loves to read and write poetry. Her favorite hobby is to collect old and out-of-print books. She has taught Sunday School for over 17 years. She is an ordained Minister and Elder of the Gospel.

Contact Information

Email: beverly.davis@sc.rr.com

Made in the USA
Middletown, DE
03 April 2023